NATIONAL GEOGRAPHIC

Ladders

TROPICAL Rain Forest ADVENTURE

Welcome to the Rain Forest

by Julia Osborne

Where can you find the greatest variety of living things? You can find it in a tropical rain forest.

If you want to visit one, travel toward the Equator. It is mostly warm there. And at least 250 cm (100 inches) of rain fall every year.

The largest rain forest in the world grows near the Amazon River in South America. Millions of plants and animals live there. Scientists have discovered many of them. Even more are yet to be discovered.

The Amazon rain forest is the largest rain forest on Earth.

The Emergent Layer

Rain forest plants grow in four different layers. The highest layer is called the **emergent layer.** Tall trees rise above the rest of the forest.

Trees in the emergent layer get the most sunlight. The weather is hot and windy. Heavy rain and lightning are common.

The harpy eagle lives in the tallest trees. It catches large monkeys. Then it eats them!

The blue morpho butterfly often flies above the treetops.

The white-throated toucan has a very large bill. Its bill helps it eat fruit, insects, and lizards.

The Canopy

Below the emergent layer is the **canopy.** It is like the roof of the forest. Tree branches and leaves grow close together. The leaves use energy from sunlight to make food for the trees.

Many animals eat the trees' leaves. They also eat their fruits and seeds. Other animals eat the animals that eat plants. Many animals that live in the canopy never go to the ground.

The canopy is the busiest layer of the rain forest. What a racket! Parrots squawk. Toucans croak. Frogs peep. Bees buzz. The wings of beetles click and whirr.

The most common animals in the canopy are insects. The most common insects are beetles. A scientist found more than 900 different kinds of beetles on just one tree!

A red howler monkey opens its mouth wide. ROAR! The monkey sounds scary. But it eats mostly leaves and fruits.

This three-toed sloth moves very s-l-o-w-l-y. It has green algae in its hair. That helps the sloth blend in with the leaves.

Some beetles of the Amazon

Tortoise beetle   Rhinoceros beetle

Jewel beetle   Rhinastus weevil

The Understory

The **understory** is below the canopy. Small trees and shrubs grow in this layer.

The canopy blocks the sunlight. This makes the understory dim. Many plants have huge leaves. These leaves capture the small amount of light that comes through the canopy.

Watch out! There are dangerous animals here. Scorpions sting. Ants bite. Spiders spin sticky webs. Powerful jaguars jump on other animals.

An emerald boa constrictor is ready to catch a bird or a mouse.

The pygmy marmoset licks the sweet sap that comes out of trees.

Poison dart frogs have poison in their skin. The poison has been used to make poisoned arrows.

Rain Forest Food Chain

The different layers of the rain forest are linked together by **food chains.** A food chain shows how energy passes from one kind of living thing to another.

The Brazil-nut tree gets energy from sunlight. It uses energy to make Brazil nuts.

The agouti gets energy by eating Brazil nuts. It is the only animal that can chew open the hard part around the Brazil nuts.

The jaguar gets energy by eating smaller animals, such as agoutis.

The green anaconda is the heaviest snake in the world. It wraps its body around its prey. Then it squeezes until its prey cannot breathe.

The Forest Floor

Did you bring a flashlight? It can be very dark on the forest floor. Only a few shrubs, ferns, and grasses grow here. Leaves, fruits, and seeds drop from the canopy. Ants and termites crawl on the ground. Fungi and bacteria break down dead things.

Surprise! Rain forest soil is not very rich. Dead things decay quickly. Nutrients from decaying plants and animals are taken up by tree roots. Few nutrients are left in the thin soil.

The Brazilian tapir has a wiggly snout. It sniffs out food. Only young tapirs have stripes.

The bird-eating tarantula can be nearly as big as a dinner plate.

A casque-headed frog opens its huge mouth. Then it snaps at an enemy.

Check In What are the four layers of the rain forest? List an animal from each layer.

Read to find out how a field biologist takes pictures of animals at night.

Tim Laman
NIGHT IN THE RAIN FOREST

by Julia Osborne

It's evening on the island of Borneo. Tim Laman is heading into the rain forest.

Why go at night? That's when many animals wake up! Tim tells us why. "At night the rain forest is as rich in life as it is by day, but with an almost completely different cast of characters."

Bats, owls, and moths hide during the day. They start moving when the sun sets. These animals are **nocturnal.** They are active at night.

Tim photographed the animals in this story. It took him many months. Often he stayed awake all night. "I went totally nocturnal for weeks, staying out in the forest until the first hint of dawn," he says.

Equator

Borneo is a huge island in the Pacific Ocean near Southeast Asia.

10

TIM LAMAN is a photographer and field biologist. He studies the wildlife in places such as rain forests and coral reefs. His photographs have won him many awards. He hopes his photos will inspire people to save rain forests and other natural places.

Perched in a tall tree, Tim gets ready to take pictures at night.

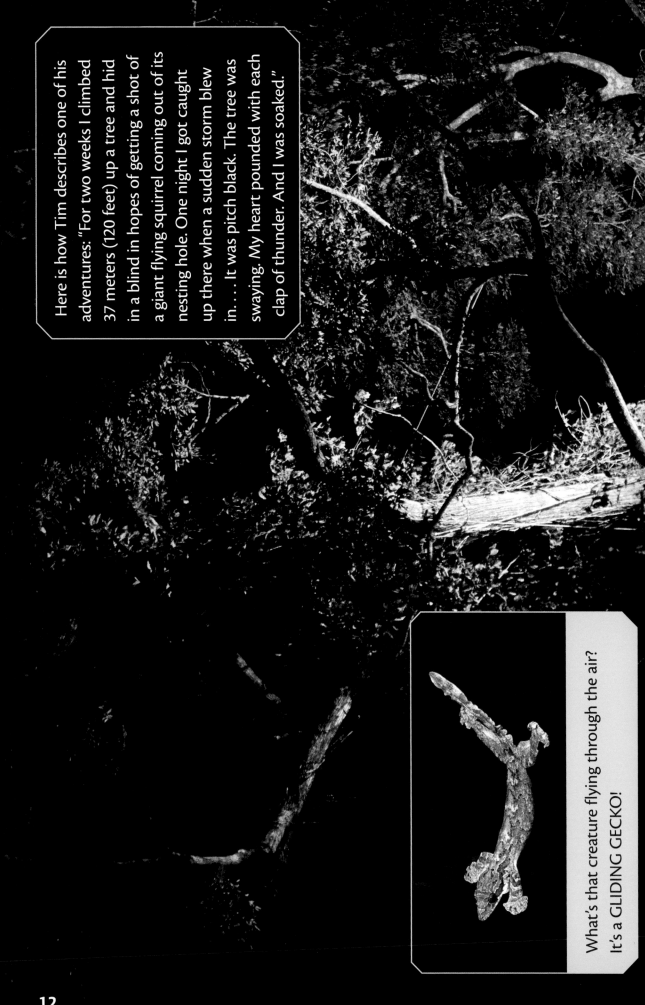

Here is how Tim describes one of his adventures: "For two weeks I climbed 37 meters (120 feet) up a tree and hid in a blind in hopes of getting a shot of a giant flying squirrel coming out of its nesting hole. One night I got caught up there when a sudden storm blew in. . . . It was pitch black. The tree was swaying. My heart pounded with each clap of thunder. And I was soaked."

What's that creature flying through the air? It's a GLIDING GECKO!

Gliding Through the Forest

Borneo has more kinds of gliding animals than any other place on Earth. These animals don't have wings. They can't really fly. They glide from tree to tree.

Gliders usually live in treetops. No one had ever taken pictures of them in action. Some people thought it would be too hard. Tim was up for the challenge.

Sometimes Tim climbed up to the **canopy.** This layer of leaves is high above the forest floor. Tim brought his cameras. He built a hiding place called a blind. Then he waited and waited. He waited for a glider to come close. Then he snapped its picture.

Tim took this picture of a Wallace's flying frog as one glided to the ground. "It was exciting to see something that very few people have seen before. To capture it on film was a real high point."

Light up the Night

What is the rain forest like at night? Tim says, "Whether I am strolling along a forest track or making a nighttime climb of a dipterocarp tree, the night has many surprises. . . . On a moonless, overcast night, I turn off my headlamp and stand among the towering trees of Borneo's lowland forest. At first it seems as black as the deepest cave. But as my eyes adjust, I see that the forest has some light of its own."

Flash! A plant hopper is captured in a nighttime photo. The long "tail" of this insect is really poop! The plant hopper feeds on plant juices. Then it releases long waxy strands of waste.

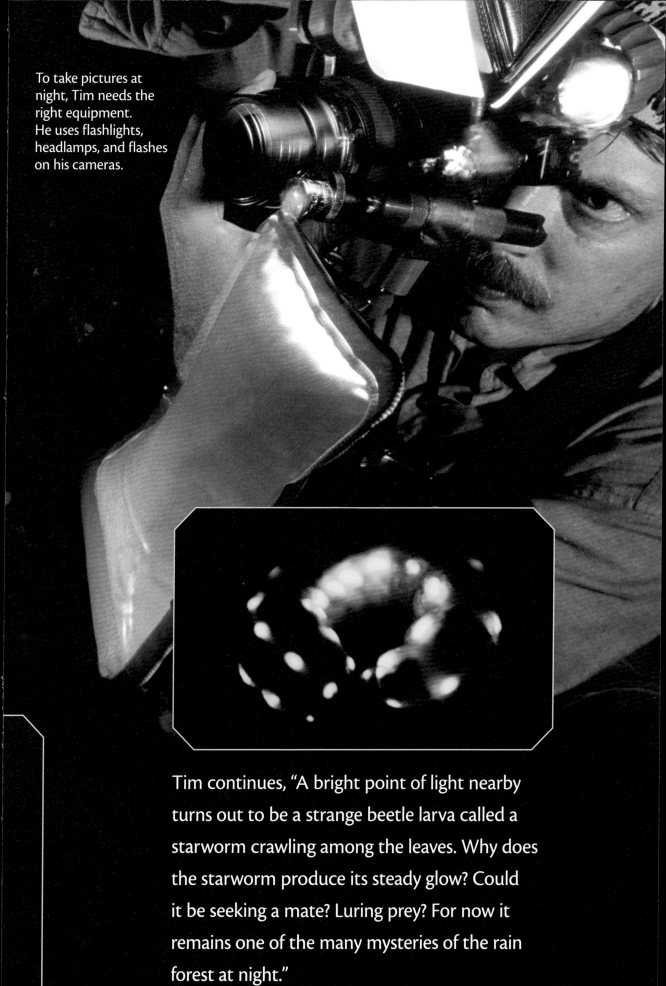

To take pictures at night, Tim needs the right equipment. He uses flashlights, headlamps, and flashes on his cameras.

Tim continues, "A bright point of light nearby turns out to be a strange beetle larva called a starworm crawling among the leaves. Why does the starworm produce its steady glow? Could it be seeking a mate? Luring prey? For now it remains one of the many mysteries of the rain forest at night."

Tim uses a bright headlamp to see a lizard.

Super Senses

How do animals survive in the dark? They use their senses. They use sight, hearing, touch, and smell. "I wish my senses were a match for these nocturnal creatures," says Tim.

"One evening as I entered the forest, I smelled a heady perfume coming from a flower opening to attract small moths. Like many night-blooming plants, this orchid has pale flowers that are easy to spot in low light."

This is a tarsier. It lives on a large island near Borneo. Tarsiers have huge eyes, sharp ears, and a delicate sense of touch. They use these senses to find food. This tarsier is eating a cockroach. Yum!

Night is ending. The nocturnal animals look for safe resting places. Some hide in dark tree holes. Others crawl into cracks in bark. They wait for darkness to return.

Tim hurries home. It's time for him to get some sleep. He hears birds greet the new day. The daytime animals are waking up!

Check In How does Tim Laman take pictures of animals at night? What equipment does he use?

Saving the Rain Forests

by Julia Osborne

Why would anyone destroy a rain forest?

Some people cut down trees to make room for crops or cattle. Others sell the wood or make paper. Still others want to build roads and cities.

Earth's rain forests are in danger. More than half of them have been cut down or burned. Scientists are worried. If this continues, the rain forests could be gone in 100 years!

We need to save our rain forests. Animals need them. People need them. They are important to the environment.

Millions of plants and animals live in rain forests. When forests are cut down, the animals have no place to live. They might go **extinct.** This means that they would no longer live on Earth.

The land is harmed when trees are cut down. There are no roots to hold the soil in place. Wind and water carry the soil away. Floods destroy farms and villages.

Products We Need

Do you like bananas and chocolate? These foods come from rain forest plants.

People who live in rain forests depend on them for food, clothing, and shelter. People around the world get food and important products from rain forests, too.

Rain forest plants are used to make medicines. These medicines help people fight diseases.

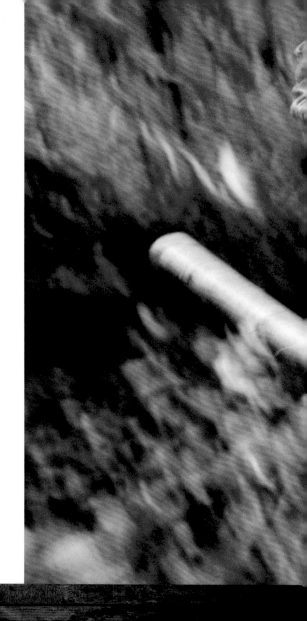

Rain Forest Products

 **Tropical fruits** such as bananas, guavas, mangoes, papayas, and passion fruit

 **Woods** such as balsa, mahogany, and teak

 **Nuts** such as Brazil nuts, cashews, kola nuts, and macadamia nuts

 **Rubber and fibers** such as bamboo, ramie, and rattan

 **Flavorings** such as cinnamon, coffee, chocolate, ginger, nutmeg, and vanilla

 **Medicines** used to treat diseases such as arthritis, cancer, diabetes, heart disease

RAINFOREST ALLIANCE
TM
CERTIFIED

Many products can be safely harvested from rain forests. **Sustainable harvesting** is safe for wildlife and people.

This seal means that a product has been harvested sustainably.

Brazil nuts can be harvested sustainably. People sell the nuts they collect from the forest floor. This saves trees. It also helps people make money.

Rain Forest Parks

Rain forests are AMAZING. Some countries set aside parts of rain forests as parks. Tourists can see the wildlife without harming the trees. Some people pay to stay in a rain forest. Their money helps the local people. It is also used to protect the forest.

Working Together

People should work together to save the world's rain forests. This will protect plants and animals from going extinct. It will help people get the products they need.

If we save our rain forests now, people will be able to enjoy them for centuries to come.

What you can do

**You can help save the rain forests.
It doesn't matter where you live.**

- Use less paper. Recycle paper.

- Buy rain forest products that have been harvested sustainably.

- Do not buy pets from rain forests.

- Share what you know about rain forests. Encourage people to help save the rain forests.

Check In How are rain forests important to people around the world?

Discuss

1. How did the information in "Welcome to the Rain Forest" help you understand the other two pieces in the book?

2. Compare the canopy layer of a rain forest with the forest floor. How are they alike and different?

3. Think about the rain forest at night. How are animals able to find food in the dark? Give some examples.

4. Explain what will happen to the rain forest animals if the trees are cut down.

5. What do you still wonder about tropical rain forests? What would be some good ways to find out more?